Until It Is True

Until It Is True

Poems by

Katy Luxem

Cover image by Nikki Watson
Cover design by Shay Culligan
Author photo by Katy Luxem

ISBN: 978-1-63980-405-4

Kelsay Books
502 South 1040 East, A-119
American Fork, Utah 84003
Kelsaybooks.com

For those who helped make it true.

Acknowledgments

Acknowledgments are given to the following publications, where I was grateful to have some of the poems in this book appear first:

The 6ress: "Wrecking Ball," "The Dreams of Your Heart Will Come True"

The Appalachian Review: "First Frost," "Daylight Savings"

Blood Moon Journal: In Bloom: "Common Names for Flowers"

Eunoia Review: "First Meal Out After Becoming Parents," "On the Eve of Your Ninth Birthday"

Free Verse Revolution Lit: "The Years Are Short"

The Mum Poem Press: Choices: "DO NOT MAKE EXTRA WORK FOR YOURSELF"

North Dakota Quarterly: "The Day My Son Learns About Death," "Recital"

Poetry Online: "How to Have Hope"

Rattle: Poets Respond: "Rumors"

Rattle: "Ways to Break My Heart"

Sky Island Journal: "Fifth-Grade PE"

SWWIM Every Day: "Stellar Contronym"

Contents

Normal day, let me be aware of the treasure you are . . .

One day I shall dig my nails into the earth or bury my face in the pillow or stretch myself taut or raise my hands to the sky and want, more than all the world, for your return.

—Mary Jean Irion

Palinode

19 / tattoo / it
on my body /
I'll never be a mother /
The world is simply too much.

Then once, twice, three times
I retract this.
I name them all beginning.

Swimming, Pregnant

Floating   snow globe fetus
      Fridays at the leisure center
face down   flip turn
      whole hemisphere of a woman
sliding through   fish-blue
      lungs, light breaking   air
goggles   leaking
      still the water
holds my weight   like the earth
      cannot. Reach
and   pull to memorize,
and remember   the feeling
of breath   and   body
lapping   one   another.

Miscarriage

I eye small jerseys at the Seahawks game,
hold one up to the belly of my life, think maybe #3?
But as if on cue, I'm running to the bathroom
in the rain, the smell of hot dogs misting sickly near
the 50-yard line. I don't know the score, but we lost
that game. I toss a mess of underwear, a baby-
sized football into a dumpster. We were going to make
waffles for dinner. We go to the beer garden instead.

How to Fall Asleep

They said to let the puppy lay on top
of a thing that smells like mama
so it learns not to howl in its sleep.
My love, you took her from a brown box
whimpering and brought her to
our bed. So, I knew you'd be an okay father
when the time came. You'd know how
to let a baby feel you breathe
skin to skin, vestiges of home.
It's all the same instinct, every creature
just wants to feel a love
so close it keeps us warm.

Things That Make the Heart Lurch with Anxiety

After Sei Shōnagon

Two-hundred and seventy-eight
days of pregnancy.
Seeing a dog limping. Broken things.
Running late. The first night home.
Cutting a watermelon.
Being needed. Needing.
Stitches and staples.
Barely pink limbs, so skinny.
Crowded parking lots.
Danger in every rearview.
Now everything means something.
This love. It could crack open
or carry me. How we are all
two versions of the same story.

Newborn

Who is carrying who? You might wonder
if you saw the mother with a confetti-print carrier,
swaying to the beat of a lost boy-band song.
She is shopping with her week-old child and unzipped
sweatshirt in the glowing produce section.
You might question how long she can do this,
and not understand that time stopped being finite
when birth broke her open. The tiny head
resting on her chest makes a space
that will be filled with white chunks. It marks her
soft cotton shirt with sweat and breath.
Then again, you might not wonder at all,
as she bags apples, weighing her aches and joy.
You may not even notice where her baby
ends and she begins.

Postpartum

For Andrew

I hold my struggle like it is my own
newborn wrapped in muslin.
When the body feels tender,
I stay away from stair railings.
When the mind aches, I stay awake
through the wide night.
Without asking, I do what I must
until the edges of a day become
weeks, become me wondering where
are my ideas? I hear you singing
to our child in the other room
and it is then I know we will survive,
for you left the door wide open.

First Meal Out After Becoming Parents

Some appetizer to the whole meal
of this new tenderness.
My breasts hugged my ribs, fat
with milk. What did we eat
that early night out?
Did your feet graze
mine under the table?
I don't remember the sunset,
or how hurried we were
as you paid the parking meter.
In my daze she is hunger
crying for me, always
some place I cannot get to.
Maybe it was tacos, lime and salt
rocks, or teriyaki bowls so fast
it was nearly take-away. I do not crave
those early days at all,
only the way I knew food never
tasted so good, so needed.

The Nature of Things

The older I get, the less I believe the story
of gravity and a falling fruit discovery.
Because women have always known
a heavy existence. Weighed down
with pregnant bodies or work somewhere
between home and a pale moon spinning.
I know because I carry bandaids
in a stained handbag, and constant worry
in my orbit. Children on my hip and iron pans
baked hard into my evenings.
Haven't we all dropped everything
and understood its path perfectly?
Maybe those women didn't say it or name it
like a wobbly child learning to walk.
Maybe they buried it in case
it bloomed and they were called a heretic.
They grew so tired and then so thankful
for a place to lay and rest,
a ground to pull them in and hold them
when nothing else made sense.

Common Names for Flowers

All buds have a genus and species,
Latin roots for both the natives and interlopers.
Because in Greece or India this bloom is different
than my suburb, but it's still the same soft pink
from my grandmother's driveway.

I name my daughters after flowers
when they're born, curvy vowels
for their fragile petal fingers.
Beautiful little things and when they speak
I hear all the perennial women:
medicinal, culinary, ornamental, essential.

They grow like the lush answer of spring,
and I tend to them but do not tame them to a fence.
I let them blossom into their abundant selves,
I do not speak any other language.

That First Year

One is just about the perfect age,
you reach for me,
two teeth are tiny sparks in your many
electric smiles,
three night wakeups only now,
but you still fit against my ribs
like it is home.
Someday I will wake up at night
alone, with nothing but hours
of quiet stretched before me.
And I will count the things
I'd trade for a moment of you
in my arms again
as I move in the darkness,
muscle memory
toward the rocking chair
that held us
together in its endless sway.

How to Comfort Anyone

Find one small arm of sunshine
even when they don't want the light
on their face. Requirements: Maybe
a fence to meet at, a door to leave
cracked. Maybe do nothing bigger
than pointing out the obvious.
I am here in the trudge of darkness.
I am listening like an enormous shadow.
And still, you are bigger than sorrow.
If on any given day you are this lonely
mountain, go ahead and be the sound.
I will be the echo.

Magic Powers

The day can be broken   into four
moments.   One, the baby
waking and needing only me. Two
parts, the rush of limbs so I don't
          remember being
cold once that winter. Three,
I google my grandma.   Find her
soup recipe is not
on the internet. Four,
                I don't know
that I love what I am doing
at this   dark hour.
But I am doing   what I love.

Good Night

He sleeps so soundly,
head ceding to a hamburger pillow,
haircut needed, body warm
and small against the dark.
I stand above him and the silence
speaks to me, says perhaps
you are a good mother
after all, look at him dreaming
of nowhere else but the softness
you have made around him.

Parenting

What do we carry but complaints
in our tender joints, aches in our oldest
ways? Even my young kids have a sore
calf or a ghrelin-spiked shine. Sometimes
I think, cry me a river. And other days
I hold the baby of them, still. Not sure
if I could ever stop caring for every ailment.
All winter I sneak into their rooms at night,
and dab cream on their chapped lips, slowly
as the air pulls in and out of their resting
faces. They do not know this and never will.
Love is a body that mothers in the dark,
a salve for any painful thing.

Mouths of Babes

I speak to my kids in simile often.
Look, the moon is like a half-eaten cookie,
sliding glass of sky, of milky stars.
The dog sleeps as a grizzly in winter.
Sadness can wash over you like a wave,
as you climb through the crest of a day.

They grow up as easily as a heart snaps,
and when they know the rules of language
they can break them, too. Now they
tell me how inexplicable the world is
and it is like our history sings.

Spell for Motherhood

One burden
    drinking through the throat
of exhaustion. A house of hours, quiet and long.

Two months ago, the school drop-off.
    Eight years ago, the line cut
and born between us, I am surprised

at the weight of her. Each day
    seasoned with need. From now on, to feel
what cannot be held.

Elegy for the Fairy Tale

They name her after the Disney princess.
My girls are too young to know
it's not even her movie. But they say her
fluffy tail is like Jasmine's long hair.
Every day this gray squirrel comes
to the sliding door and sits twitching,
nosing closer and closer until it's pressed into
the house like a family member. I buy
salted peanuts, my daughter
tells her teacher it's our pet,
opens her hand full of corn kernels
in the fall. Whatever we have,
she wants. By winter, I worry for her
like I'd worry for a child. I put out
extra treats before night comes, always preparing
for loss. What kind of person feeds a squirrel?
The neighbor asks. And I keep silent
as a little rodent. Until one day she is
gone, no longer pawing at our dirty glass.
My oldest says a magic carpet took her,
and I gently unravel a fairy tale,
putting her to bed. In the long dark of it
where nothing comes, we know spring looms.
Soon, we will let go. And then we can
find the shells she left in our garden.

The Last Time I Carried You

I am afraid of the day you will be too big.
That your last time down
the twisty yellow slide was a summer day
I cannot remember. But I know you
landed on the other side
of a season that slipped away.
How cruel we get to remember
firsts and not lasts, when both ache equally.

Once, we walked a rocky beach path.
I took you off my hip because you bent
and swayed, a current too strong to be carried.
I clasped your starfish hand in mine,
which felt vast as an ocean.
You were just big enough to float
along beside me, to not let go.

DO NOT MAKE EXTRA WORK FOR
YOURSELF

—My fortune cookie, the week before I turn 35

I have made three kids
(more if you count loss) I have pulled
puppies from free classifieds
and made them soft, a cat from
the dumpster at my husband's work.
I know when the milk expires,
what a sunrise-color light
on the car dash means when it flickers
SOS. It's the driest winter in a generation
and yet the sky is blue like water,
so I take that worry on my plate too.
My father calls as I'm washing dishes,
it has been months since we talked, years
since I saw him, but he does not ever forget
birthdays. He asks if I fell off
the face of the earth? I sigh and hold
the phone with my face and no hands
my axis tipping and I say no,
that I am here. That I am making it turn.

Walking the Dogs in January After an Argument

The cold is bare as empty branches with nothing
between them but air and loss tonight.
When somewhere in the open winter field
your hand reaches for mine. I feel the heat
where we touch, even through our gloves.

Two Tooth Fairies

That night, there were two tooth fairies.
One in lightweight Birkenstocks with a dog
following into our daughter's room. She had
lost a molar, and I plucked it from the gummy
pillow and replaced it with three bills folded
in on each other. Then came my husband,
later and diligently unaware, to make sure
the task was complete. Two ones, enough
for a whole need to be filled. How lucky,
I thought, to have so much. Knowing I had
a dad, of course, and he was somewhere.
But never in my room at night, in the warm
shaft of light at the door. Never giving wings
to my fantasy. Never filling in the gap
or space of when he left, empty-handed,
taking so many small things with him.

Field Guide for the Western Mom

Virtually every mother's range
is the nest, the minivan, the backpack
which must be emptied for food storage
lest they starve. Only she knows
the edges of toddler boredom and rage.
She is able to distinguish the child's favorite rock
once collected and found in the washing machine
in a denim pocket. Only she has a body
made to sustain, a softness to carry
offspring and their multitude
of belongings. Look how she saves
the art and fact of it, the first haircut tousled,
feathers in a clear baggie. She understands
time is endangered, habitat loss
keeps her upright at odd hours.
She is a warbler, a worker bird,
she is the west and the east
for all who call to her.

In Praise of the Late Spring Snow

The mountains cut wedges
of sky and my son, insulated
in boots but with bright bare legs,
is caught in flakes and puddles
of runoff. Everything is green
for a moment on this little umbrella
edge of April. What is leaving
and what is staying? And who
can say what hand holds
this specific tenderness in
the driveway? We'll go back
inside. Unsure of what hat
to wear in the cold light. A new
muse, and yet the same as always.

Written During a War

The daffodils with their eyelashes blinking
at the border, a flash expanse of yellow
to the battered winter blanket of our
front lawn. Patchy quilt of blades
laid down flat against the March
air, to think each lithe leaf must have
surrendered like backcountry skiers
in an avalanche of late snow. But here
the flowers come opening anyway
like they know something even when
it cannot be guaranteed. To believe
the dormant grass will come back.
To give anything to see it.

Yard Work

Bent as an agile stem,
the memory of my little daughter,
with her pink face and toddler toes
eager like earthworms in the dirt,
blooms each spring on schedule.
Some brightness pulls me outside
of the blue house, shows me
the way to weed and till softly.
Not hunter or gatherer, not wayward
with hunger, but settler in my own life,
my body of work in these raised beds.
We'll bring forth a tomato to salt,
the rosemary that just won't quit,
a single green serrano the size
of a small open palm. To know
the rain will come is transformative
enough. A sudden break in the clouds
makes me grateful, knowing
we'll plant the garden soon.

Recital

After the bow, after the cheering faded
we gave her flowers like little spotlights.
Crinkling cellophane peeled away
cheap carnations soft as a blushed cheek,
she took home the ballet-shoe
buds and the tender pink petals
lifted high on stem arms like a dancer.

Still, they fell. The vase only holding
fresh stems so long, we said goodbye.
But she cherished them too much
and haven't we all tried
to keep something alive that would die?
I tossed them once wilted,
but she'd kept some. Petals tucked
under her pillow so when night bloomed
around us, I saw a garden
tangled in her hair.

Wrecking Ball

For years, my toddler daughters called
Miley Cyrus, "Wrecking Ball."
It was a compliment, a proper noun
for the way powerful women defy structure.
They'd see her on the cover of a magazine
and say, there's my favorite singer,
     Wrecking Ball.
They'd put on pink Doc Martens and crash
around landing on twin beds
with all their passion unchained.
There's still a lesson in the way
they name things for an icon of demolition.
There's still a crack in their bedroom drywall,
more visible than a glass ceiling.

Do You Hate Me?

My daughter asks, she is angry at me
because I said there is not time
for video games right now.
But I helped her with her paper
about an American hero.
Don't you see? The real world needs building,
not fake blocks and hours lost.
I got her mozzarella sticks for lunch,
because they are her favorite
and I did not forget the sauce.
I found her gloves, I washed her
jewel-colored coat and dried it
so she will stay warm when I
take her to her horse
riding lesson. But I cannot make her
drink from my love that easily.
It is not what I do for her
that she sees. It is when I break
she remembers. And when she goes
running off with an innate car door slam,
I hold her jacket for the longest time.

The ending line is in conversation with the ending line of "Little Beast" by Richard Siken.

43

Contronym Three Ways

My father and I mostly
talk about the weather.
When was the last snow?
How warm is it where you are?
Our sky is the same, I suppose
always has been barely blue,
connecting earth to space
or Montana and Salt Lake.
What is there to say now
after all of these years?
His memories are leaving
as if I am 8 and he is breezing
out the door for good. To weather
a lifetime of his path is to know a storm
leaves more than wreckage.
I am weathered down. I might say
nothing is new here; what I mean
is the sun may still come out.

Three Under Five

We go to bed
too exhausted
to do anything else
but lightly graze
fingertips before
welcoming sleep
as if it were a lover.

Family Dinner

In between reading about corgis and mermaids,
between bikes and dolls with shocks of blue hair,
you hear snippets of news. A mugging, a murder
is a slow death of innocence. You make Sims
have a fake family, build a house, but we do
not keep out the inseam of knowledge
and I see how grief lengthens you.
The zipper on your coat breaks,
so you notice what I can't fix;
there's not always an answer
and life is metal teeth held
at your tender neck. So,
we arrive to dinner,
table the speaking
of an end, exhale,
and begin
to eat.

Returning from a Weekend Trip to New Orleans

What would it be like
to have an airport
access road named
after you? I see small things
in their places. A mailbox
shingled without reason,
on this strange street.
How we go
on after flying
across time zones
to taste the king cake
colors of another city.
A baby reminds me
of mine. A thousand
miles from here
their hands wait
for souvenirs.
Why do we go
someplace
foreign? To make
home again
a destination.

On the Eve of Your Ninth Birthday

Your room faces the front of the house
where the streetlights make shadows
like strangers on your wall. Sometimes
you run in bad-dream panic to find me asleep,
not soundly. And so I tell you the story
of your birthday: How you refused
to come when I asked. How we didn't know
who you were at all, but when we saw
your little chin quivering with the disturbance
of that first light, we said there is
our beautiful daughter. And we held
our hopes to her like hands
and rocked her to sleep.

COMPETENCE LIKE YOURS IS UNDERRATED

—Fortune cookie fortune on a Tuesday

There are days
when I cannot do anything
right. And yet
the hours only go
as far as I take them.

The Day My Son Learns About Death

He is five and eating dinner,
we have perhaps said the word *pandemic*
too many times in the last year.
Tears the size of peas season his plate.
He asks if we will be a thousand years old.
He asks if it will be summer then.
When it happens, will we miss each other?

My son, how do I answer the unimaginable?
I think of my grandmother,
her rings glinting in the last days
of April. All I want is to tell you that yes,
the sun shines. How it is like when
I pick you up from preschool. Without fail,
I always arrive and you run to me.
Do not be sad, I want to say,
it will be like coming home.

Funeral

I take my kids
up the canyon
to find the biggest leaf
palm-wide and deep
with orange and earth
dropped and footfall crisp.
We do not mourn
this small death
in fact
when the woods come alive
we take in their joy.

Seasons

Tonight, for the last time
I read my daughter a picture book.
It is cold out now, but my voice
is warm and soft.
I tuck the blankets up
over her long body,
clouds hugging the mountains.
The book is about seasons
changing color, crisp air,
the green and syrup of trees.
And in real life, it is autumn
so time does what it does.
The wind powers through our street,
it blows away the leaves.

Daylight Savings

When pulling the dead flowers free, I stopped time
for a moment to notice the losing sunlight. Loose dirt
shook off like the hours of the day. The darkness
came early, shaded by the mountain so there was no
edge to it. I dragged the bodies away. I didn't
notice the seeds scatter like migrating birds headed to the
warm center of our earth. May they wait the long winter
for a precarious spring. May I forget them in the night,
as a dream flies elsewhere. Until the sun rises early,
a marigold waiting for me on the other side.

How to Have Hope

There must be something wrong with me.
In the fall, the neighbors spray their eaves,
with poison dripping like a soft rain. They'd kill
for a weedless lawn, a pest-free porch.
But I sit outside thinking the light is honey
for us all. I'll leave the sunflowers
until they freeze, and let my many-legged
thoughts go. Part of me is always hurting
for the smallest among the living. I can't help
how I open, instead of shut before winter.
I leave a crack. I invite the spiders in.

Worship

Sunday comes and it is always
a miracle. Not because of god,
but because there is nothing
we believe in except our ability
to get by, together. Is it not a miracle
we made it through another week
happy? The pantry stocked
with fruit leather, words at our throat
a sticky gift, the light at the window
a forehead kiss. And you by my side
folding school uniforms, running a bath,
holding us together hour by hour.
Divorce me from anything holy
that is not here, for this is my religion.

First Frost

The snow line on the mountain
is crisp and white, easing down
to swallow autumn like a ripe apple.

One day we wake to find
the yard full of deer, antlers
pointing every direction. A pair
searching for warmth in the glaze
of once-sweet grass.

It has been a long time since
a doe appeared this close. I think
they must be hungry now.
Or, how nothing we know
really ever leaves us.

Sometimes We Write Together

The dog and I in the office.
I hold our burdens, like the work
of a plain Tuesday, the unfilled form,
list what we'll eat later for dinner.
Nothing is for him and yet
everything is for him too.
But he mainly remembers winter
and the spill of snow on the grass.
No thinking, just running on instinct.
Perhaps that's the way to do it,
one of us here, and the other always
elsewhere. His tail a melodic compass
toward sticks and leaves and joy.

Year 15 of Marriage

Hot-water bottle filled each night
and placed in our daughter's sheets.
In the morning, the tea ready
steeped to the temperature of us.
Lit fire behind the glass of our living
room, another month goes by
and the bills are paid
to heat the spaces in this big house.
Still, when it's below zero
and my husband comes to me
in our bed, when it's late winter
and the blankets cannot do enough—
He finds my body, knows the way
to warm it too.

December 24

Waking, my husband says
Isn't this your favorite
day of the entire year?
And then kisses me
with all of my anticipation.

Nourishment

I was so weary of this year by Christmas
that I thought to gift you a poem
like an orange you'd find in the toe
of your stocking. Which surprises
and sweetens you without meaning to,
as you cup it in your curved palm,
when you peel it into soft segments,
as the fresh juices fill your mouth,
a sunshine into your very bones.

December 26

A day ago, I washed
with egg the shapes
we most identified with.
Wreath, cactus, tree,
everything to hold icing
and berries and thorns.
In the dark
light of the kitchen
I taste ginger and
think of winter, the months
cut out behind us.
Before the end,
to know the flavor
of what loves us back.
Then to swallow
the whole year.

Let Me Say Thank You

It's all I have to bring to-day, This and my heart, beside,
This, and my heart, and all the fields . . .
—Emily Dickinson

I said this quote meant a lot to me
and you opened your hunger like a dream
brings, one I cannot help having.
You and I ate life as a reaper might.
We had children and Christmas
trees. We had popcorn and melon
in the summer and dogs on leashes,
the barely contained exuberance.
Mostly I worried about things
I could not control. Mostly you held
my hand and my heart wherever
we laid down together. I got up
at night, lonely or cold and there
you were. Holding your phone's light
toward the door, a path where before
I could see only the moon.

When My Children Were Small

The weeks of their birthdays
we lit candles a thousand times.
Every meal, it seemed a celebration.
Licked frosting off the bottom
of a matchstick and whipped cream
off their tiny fingers. Pancakes
and cheesecake slices and layers
eaten as they sang at every meal,
happy birthday and cumpleaños feliz,
and some silly verses they must have
learned at school or else without me.
I watched rainbow wax rivulets slide
onto cold plates and harden
like joy. Perhaps if we kept some
spark of it going, the light
might move with us into another year.

What Love Is

A snowstorm smothered the yard night and day
and night again. Flakes weighed on the eaves, patio
furniture and even heavy cars. Inches and then feet deep.
I think of how you knew to go out, even in such cold
when the world sat quietly muffled against itself.
You, bundled up in the icy morning light, gently shaking
the boughs of our little peach tree until all the branches
were free of snow. How tenderly your flame burned
away this burden, so the tree stayed upright and strong.
It is both unremarkable and a complete miracle
that spring ever arrives. And how often.

The Source

My son sees a globe like it is a balloon
rising. Grasps the mountains as if they're braille,
feels a dream out of words like *gouda*
and *arigato.* He asks how far to Brazil,
how many hours on a plane to Iran,
is there a boat to Arizona? Here is the earth
in his throat like a first-grade Spanish lesson,
the Great Wall of still-unknown length. A bird's
eye peering at a loaded dumpster in an alley
in France. For every place he hasn't been,
he has a string wrapped in his fist. To live
is to wonder and to ask again and again:
How many holds does the world have on you?

Ode to the Pocket of Air in My Sheets

And by my thighs.
It is spring.
Someone has left
the window open.

Post-Swim

I can hear a whole ocean,
or at least the want of a return,
water in the ears, a jostling
of shells, a far-off wave
of pain, coming like age
like the sound of inhaled breath
before going under.

I spray sunscreen on the body, glazed
donut skin that isn't a shape I thought
possible, but swims anyway.
Now the years are tan lines, easy
to notice on the hip of an afternoon.

My kids are young and beautiful,
they take the diving jewels
I bought and toss them,
weighted and clinking on the bottom
of the pool. I tip my head,
watching how far they dive,
deeper and deeper now until
nothing can come out.

Would You Like to Join My 4-Week Gut-Health Program?

No, it's nearly July
and I'll wear dresses
so nothing cuts
my body in two, nothing
stops the full breeze
from billowing out
like soft, heavy curtains.
Give me dough and pastry
and in Paris, two weeks
of what must be essential
gluten. And my son
with watermelon juice
dripping down his chin,
saying the strawberries
are almost ripe, are ready
for the taking.

French Countryside, July

The raspberries ripen and the days
are so long now. I've had so much
wine, I no longer look up at the stars
and feel only the solid ground.

On Regret

It is as if I am carrying something
heavy that I can hold only so long
before setting it down and breathing
deeply. I cannot go back, but if I could,
I know I would fill your arms with flowers.

No Girl Has All Five

My daughter makes a solar oven, breaks a claw
clip and calls a boy at the park *brah.* She opens
a bank account that gives $20 for each A.
She has the height of our ancestors, the horoscope
of dark matter in deepest space. Doesn't know
how cliche it is to say women can't parallel park.
She is a straw, if love were like chocolate milk.
An enigma and the reason I don't sleep at night.
The things I know nothing of. The things I know
for sure. Prove me wrong. Prove me wrong.

We Follow the Same Accounts

I meet my husband online
often. Scroll the streets

of us: Two palms with margaritas
in hand, me pregnant, him walking

the dog. Another year or meme,
now in teacups waiting to spin.

In real life we are sometimes
ships passing in the night.

Other times I see his likes, a heart
on the screen, lowered as if he speaks

my name. Whispers, and I almost feel
his cheek, where it would touch.

I Don't Want Anything Curated by Influencers

But tell me your top picks for camping,
where to view the Milky Way unspoiled by anything
except a thick quarter of moon. How you are
no nearer to god than the blackberries and flies,
accepting whatever the end of summer offers.
What scares you? The things that happened
no more than once, the effect of your babies
on your heart and heavy pepper on your eggs.
Your recommendation for laying on a shoulder
or how it feels to long so mightily for answers
when you are both the cloud and endless sky.
What else can you endorse? When this thing
of a million things is living? Is all that there is.

Late August

We move across the country
embracing change like a species
flying south. Here, the rain stops.
The gas is cheaper. From our new
road we drive into the canyon
and see mountains spread
like open wings around us.
My husband feeds the birds
and they nourish a hot breeze
with a spray of seeds.
We do not always notice
what faces the sun,
turning golden each evening.
In cement cracks, along busted
fences, playing in dusty alleyways,
sunflowers grow everywhere.
As tall as kids, as wild as weeds.

Hymn

Originally, to honor the gods.
But what is adoration without first
a lived experience? Praise
the early apples, that Earth
is a woman. The holy sunshine
or soft summer rain. A melody
your grandfather whistled.
The waitress who gives
your son a one-dollar coin,
a treasure in his hand
when it opens warmly, an offering.
Now, to name the things
you feel. To lift them as a song.

Metaphors for Love

I taught my daughter how to whisk
crepe batter until it's smooth
and we are hungry. Not all mothers
show affection through touch,
so when I hold her small hand
over a sturdy handle, we try,
we go in circles. My mother
handed this recipe down
from hers, and showed me how
we pull the best thing toward us
again and again,
until it is filled with air.

Obstacles

For the summer I spent several hours
a week at the obstacle gym,
I have memories of watching my son
climb a rope ladder, jump to red and black
mats like a creature, rather than a little boy.

I sat in the air conditioning with my book,
and imagined telling him about it
someday. Without any idea of what age
might hold in its hot little hands.

How he wore a plastic medal
around his neck. How he told me
they might really mistake him for a ninja
when he was this sweaty.
What wall he might climb
today. If he could please stay,
just a little bit longer.

My Son Walks into the Men's Bathroom

Grocery store, a heavy wooden door,
Blues Traveler on the PA system.
Tricky locks through to plumbed

porcelain, his smooth skin and messy hair.
His stretchy waistband and a half
-tucked polo shirt of baby sky, small

functional pockets for his strange treasures.
He measured himself yesterday against our wall
inching up childhood like a soft

hug, tall enough for certain roller coasters and
every day, he looks back over his shoulder a little
less. A little less he waves in the distance

between us, as I stand by the deli, harmonica
and urinals swirling. And he goes alone now,
off to all the places I cannot follow.

Stellar Contronym

When something is exceptionally
good in life, perhaps the fried zucchini
slices of late summer or the garden,
beautiful as it is, but still a backdrop
to the evening sky, when the sun dips
its oil lamp past the horizon, perhaps then.
When I get to kiss the constellation
of a body late at night, pressed into the dark
face of gravity, as if it is a whole universe
made just for me. The glow of this luck may
make me feel faint, temporary, outstanding.
The stars are out. And the stars are out.
There is no trick to the light.

Fishing

Me and my husband with the kids
casting among the sunbaked rocks
all afternoon. I'm not a tiger mom, actually
not carnivorous at all. Instead, I untangle line
after thin line, hydrate them and open
salted pistachios, discuss the dragonfly
heartbeat and trout mouth. In it I remember
each of their entries to the world similarly.
The catch of atmosphere and adrenaline
as it happens could be death or beginning.
My little daughter had shiny skin
slick in the wet light. Her mouth agape
and pulling in life. Now she is catching
a rainbow as it flails in the same unfamiliar
air. My husband unhooks and cuts us gently
loose. None of this is for us to keep,
so we merely show reverence for the moment
with our own breath and release it.

How to Breathe

To see a large cottonwood tree,
lush and verdant even in July
bolstered by tufts of cotton
cloud on the ground like an unmade bed.
To sit back and notice the shape against
a palette of calm sky.
To know this is your favorite tree,
white bark and wind the loudest
quiet you ever heard.
To see it sigh with movement
the way a flower opens
and understand that everything has lungs.

Ways to Break My Heart

The first day of school, the small
clean shoes. A trail of glitter from the new

backpack. The pieces of us we cannot hold
onto. My mother texts, remember

when you were this age? Waist-high,
wide-eyed. Look at them go, and now my last

baby is a kindergarten name tag. Do not miss me,
I am with you. Somewhere in a long, polished hall

stop and think of me. As the years go on
and on. Open your lunchbox, I have made you

a tuna sandwich, the way you like. The crusts cut off.

Fifth-Grade PE

Today she tells me the rules
of tug-o-war, and how it takes
so many hands on the rope to win.
I listen and feel the hard pull
of years I don't know yet.
First, it was girls versus boys
then small versus big. Almost every time
it was a draw and her hands now
are red and pleated like a school skirt.
In the end, she says,
you have to use your whole body,
dig in with thighs like a dandelion
in the very field you stand on.
And then it's merely who can
hold on the longest.

Home Alone

I am eating an almond croissant
on a clean, blue plate
for the first time in years,
I hear nothing but the wind
against my door, a car passing
through the snow-filled road
out there, my children are elsewhere
and though they will return,
the intervals lengthen like femurs
and of course, there is no guarantee
but I know their secrets and they know
mine—how I still sway gently
when holding laundry or other
9-pound things, though it has been
nearly a decade since I carried
a newborn against my body,
which seems huge and yet
unremarkable, the way a memory
becomes a life, standing
in a quiet hallway
until it is real,
until it is true.

Looking for Love?

Oh, sloppy search and rescue party,
think of all the things you've found without
a map. The estate-sale plates and candles
smelling of heat soft as Arizona winter. The good
sheets. The feel of an animal near your leg. Small
corners with big windows, perfect for reading
alone. What you have carried, what you have had
to put down. How the sun is a bright lemon
in your water, a promise you drink in.
That the day has found you, again, begs
you not to worry, only to be there. Think
of all the horizons not tilted toward the space
of loss. Where you are the axis, instead.
Do that instead.

Ways I Pray

With closed eyes to a headache, when the darkness
flashes bright spots of stars all around me.
While eating enchiladas on the covered patio. As I think be
still, this is life. In disbelief at the pain and luck of it.
Sometimes, crying in the shower. When news comes
like rain, or gods flooding in. The summer my son grows
four inches. In moments that time stands still and tall.
Bowing to kiss the top of his head. When the sky is low
and limitless. To notice we exist at all in a storm.
When I do not stay asleep to the world.

Looking at a Photo from 10 Years Ago

That corner of life is folded paper
now, and the world is surely warmer.
We live in a whole different part of it, but still,
I worried so much then. My body tender
from two kids in two years. Those girls brought
out the woman in me. It was some summer
morning. And they were always needing
touch and bringing me crushed berries
that would stop my heart until I knew it wasn't
blood. My daughter, barely thigh-high
in a wading pool so wide around her
we couldn't even fill it halfway. I was
so tired that day. But the new ferns grew
wildly and the bamboo provided ample shade.
I can almost hear her laugh filtering
through baby teeth. And the lushness
of a little thing held right here in front of me.
How green the grass was.

THE DREAMS OF YOUR HEART WILL
COME TRUE

—Fortune cookie fortune on Valentine's Day

I wake sweaty and disturbed by confusion
handed to me by sleep.
Your fingers startle me until their grasp
is (again) familiar in mine,
and my panic fades, my heartbeat slows.
Or who can tell? Maybe it is yours
next to me in the dark—
a sound I did not know I listened for.

On Writing a Poem on Motherhood

A sturdy tree across the street left to grow
fast for ample, useful shade. And now
in late September, full to bursting
with heavy leaves. The mess of color before
letting go again. Always to the bare-armed
strength mustered for the winter.
She shakes her head as if she cannot
believe in this life. And from a certain height,
there must be a number of details. I know
all those, the ones she keeps only for herself.

My Daughter Asks What French Kissing Feels Like

And I don't think of fireworks, but cinnamon Altoids
sucking the scent of dinner from lips before
I taste them. I have opened my heart like the small
flowers parting all summer. Like a god,
if there was one. My mouth made me
a mother before any of her existed.
Spoke and explained. Love is a deity. I understand
the grind has teeth to it. The same day,
my daughter asks, what is an anthology?
I collect these questions and bind them
with her wonder, with a thousand answers
for you. I could write that for you.

Rumors

Someone gets mad. A boy
brings a gun to school
and plans to use it
seventh period. At the end
of the day, the bell sounds.
My daughter runs to the car
like a shot. Leaving
books and questions in her
locker. I hug her
under the crooked cherry,
where blossoms flurry.
It's so hard to believe
the trees grow this way.

Eleven

For Rosemary

When you have forgotten your first peach
walled room, and the puddles
you jumped in at our first house.
When you put your small Elmo in a box
for safe keeping, making a home of your life,
tucking messy art away with childhood
and wonder if you're good enough
for middle school, the sleepover, for Broadway,
patient enough at anything
singular to warrant the years
of hard work ahead. Asking,
what is it you'll give to this world?
Remember that I know
something you do not.
To so many things, you are the question.
To so many things, you are the answer.

About the Author

Katy Luxem grew up in Seattle and studied creative writing at the University of Washington. She has a master's degree in business from the University of Utah. Her writing has appeared in *Rattle, McSweeney's Internet Tendency, Poetry Online, The National Poetry Review, The Appalachian Review, SWWIM Every Day,* and others. *Until It Is True* is her first book. She lives in Salt Lake City with her husband and three kids.

Find her at:
www.katyluxem.com